VOTING
A Kid's Guide

by Nel Yomtov

CAPSTONE PRESS
a capstone imprint

Captivate is published by Capstone Press, an imprint of Capstone.
1710 Roe Crest Drive,
North Mankato, Minnesota 56003
www.capstonepub.com

Copyright © 2020 by Capstone. All rights reserved. No part of this publication may be reproduced in whole or in part, or stored in a retrieval system, or transmitted in any form or by any means, electronic, mechanical, photocopying, recording, or otherwise, without written permission of the publisher.

Library of Congress Cataloging-in-Publication data is available on the Library of Congress website.
ISBN 978-1-5435-9139-2 (library binding)
ISBN 978-1-4966-6603-1 (paperback)
ISBN 978-1-5435-9143-9 (eBook PDF)

Summary: Gives facts about voting, why it's important, and how it plays a part in U.S. elections.

Image Credits
Alamy: All Canada Photos, 9, Jeffrey Isaac Greenberg 1, 26; Library of Congress Prints and Photographs, 7; NASA, 23; Newscom: Joe Sohm Visions of America, 27, TNS/Al Diaz, 16-17, ZUMA Press/Paul Christian Gordon, 14; Shutterstock: Carol A Hudson, 21, eurobanks, 18, Everett Historical, 6, eyerazor, 19, Jane Kelly, 1, Joseph Sohm, 10, 13, 22, 28, 29, lightyear studio, Cover, Lost_in_the_Midwest, 11, Monkey Business Images, 24, 25, Onur ERSIN, 5, Rob Crandall, 12, 20, Sheila Fitzgerald, 15, Simone Hogan, 4, Susan Schmitz, 8

Design Elements
Capstone; Shutterstock: openeyed

Editorial Credits
Editor: Michelle Parkin; Designer: Bobbie Nuytten;
Media Researcher: Jo Miller; Production Specialist: Laura Manthe

All internet sites appearing in back matter were available and accurate when this book was sent to press.

Table of Contents

Why Is Voting Important? 4

Who Do We Vote For? 8

Spreading the Word 14

Time to Vote! 20

When You Can't Vote Yet 24

    Glossary 30
    Read More 31
    Internet Sites 31
    Index 32

Glossary terms are **bold** on first use.

Why Is Voting Important?

You may have heard your parents talk about who they want to vote for in the next election. Maybe you've talked about voting in school. Do you know why voting is so important? Voting is how we choose our leaders and make laws. It gives us the chance to say what we think about issues that affect us, such as our education or the environment.

Certain laws protect our **right** to vote. America's early leaders wanted the people to decide how the government should be run. This type of government is called a **democracy**. To do this, these men wrote the U.S. **Constitution**. The Constitution gives certain rights to the people. The right to vote is one of them.

the U.S. Constitution

At first, only some Americans could vote. Voters had to be white men. They had to be at least 21 years old. They also had to own land. Women and black Americans couldn't vote. They didn't have a say in their own government. These groups fought for voting rights.

The 15th **Amendment** was added to the Constitution in 1870. This gave black men the right to vote. But women couldn't legally vote until 1921. This is when the 19th Amendment was added. Today, voting rules have changed. A person must be at least 18 years old to vote. He or she must also be a U.S. **citizen**.

FACT: People in Belgium *have* to vote. If they don't, they could be fined. They may even lose their right to vote for up to 10 years!

President Ulysses S. Grant (center) signed the 15th Amendment into law.

Who Do We Vote For?

People vote for their senators, representatives, and the president of the United States. But it's also important to vote in your community. But why? Think about your school. Who decided to build it? Who decided that you would go to that school instead of another one? Leaders in your community decided these things. But they represent the people. Voters elected the leaders.

People vote for leaders and changes in their community.

Now imagine that you want a new ice rink built in your town. Two people are running for mayor in the next election. One of them wants to build the rink. The other does not. Which one would you vote for? When people decide not to vote, they let someone else make decisions for them.

When you vote for officials in your county or city, you are voting in a local election. Local elections can be held at different times during the year. Voters are asked to choose the mayor, police chief, and city council members.

A man voted in Ventura County, California, in 2016.

There are also state elections. Voters select their state's governor. Governors are elected every four years. Voters can also vote for the attorney general, state legislature, judges, and other state jobs.

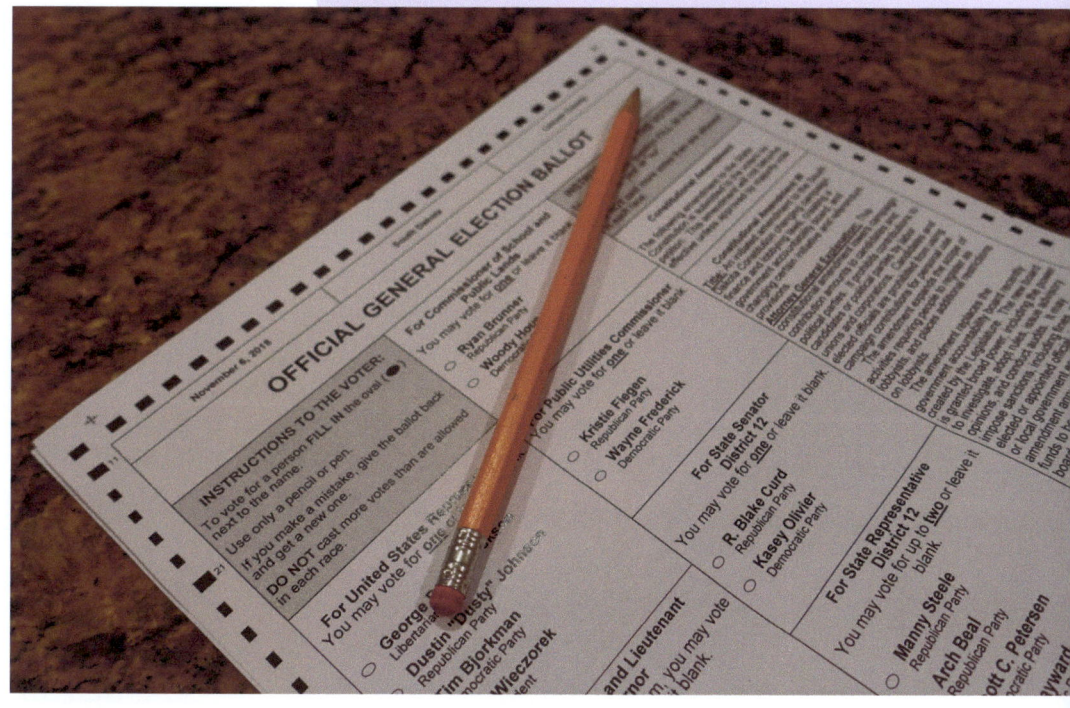

People vote for candidates on voter ballots.

FACT: People also vote on referendums in local elections. A referendum is a public vote on one important issue.

People also vote in national elections. We vote for the president and vice president every four years on Election Day. Election Day is always the first Tuesday in November in an election year. The president and vice president run as a team. They cannot be elected separately.

People in Arlington, Virginia, voted for president in 2016.

Voters also elect people in **Congress**. They vote for senators and representatives. These people represent their state and its citizens in government. Elections for senators and representatives are held every two years.

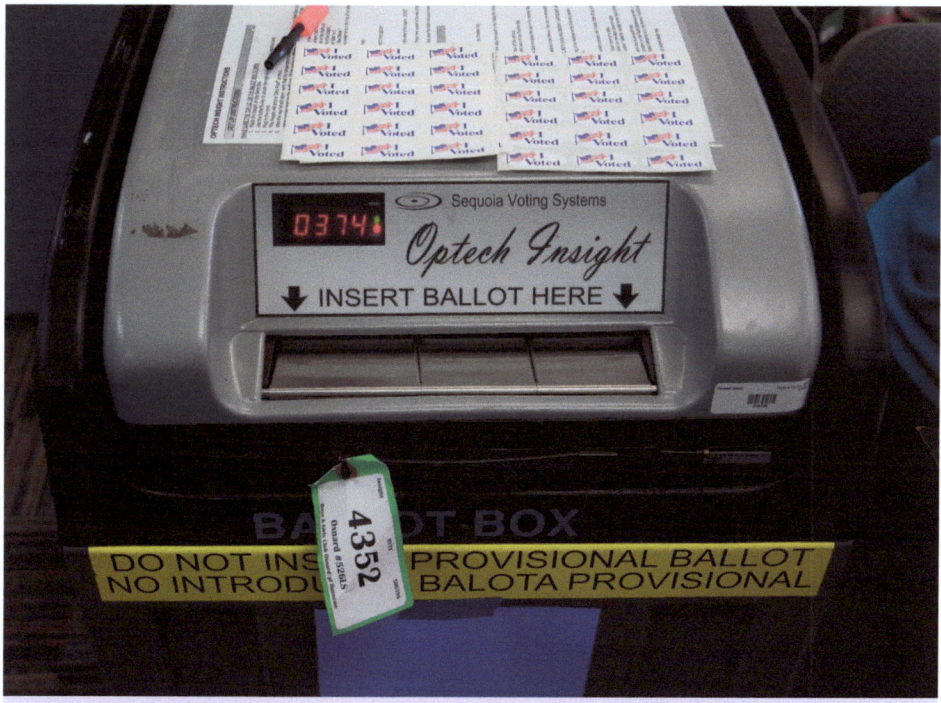

A voting machine collected the votes at a polling station in California.

Spreading the Word

During an election year, you'll see and hear a lot about people running for office. These people are called **candidates**. The candidates want voters to know who they are and what issues they believe in. They work to get people to vote for them.

Candidate Bob Hasegawa spoke to a volunteer during his campaign for mayor in 2017.

Presidential candidate Bernie Sanders spoke at his rally in 2019.

A lot of people work on a candidate's **campaign**. They hold **fund-raisers**, create ads, and mail information to voters. Some campaign workers even go door-to-door for their candidates.

There are also rallies during campaigns. People who support the candidate gather and listen to speakers. Community leaders, celebrities, and the candidates themselves speak at the rallies. These meetings are exciting events with music.

Candidates also use TV and online ads to spread their message. They have websites and social media pages to address voters. Ads can be negative or positive. Sometimes statements in the ads are not true. It's important for voters to research the facts about each candidate.

Presidential candidates debate each other in June 2019.

Candidates often have **debates** on TV. During a debate, candidates who are running for the same job are asked questions. These questions are about issues that voters care about. Voters can learn about each candidate's views during debates.

Political Parties

Political parties are groups of people who share the same views about how the government should be run. They pick candidates to represent their parties. They raise money for these candidates to run for office. Their goal is to have their candidates elected. That way, a party's goals and policies will be carried out. Two main political parties are the Democratic Party and the Republican Party.

Voters can vote for Democratic, Republican, or Independent candidates, as well as people from other parties.

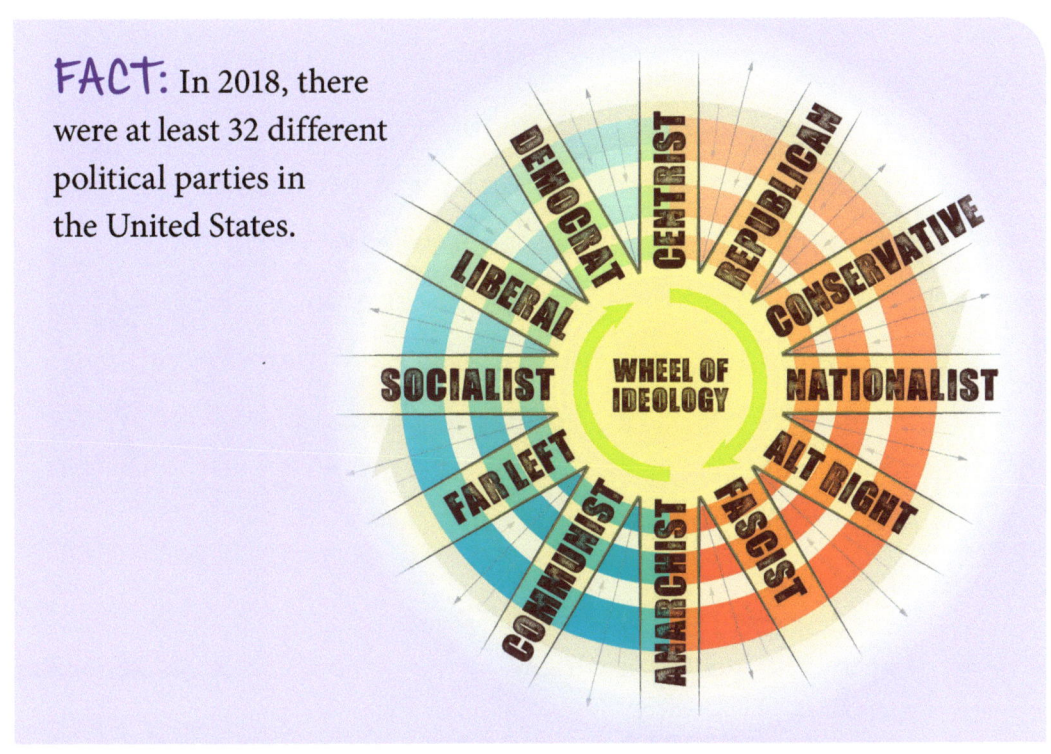

FACT: In 2018, there were at least 32 different political parties in the United States.

FUN AT THE PARTY

There have been many political parties throughout America's history. In 1940, a husband and wife comedy team started the Surprise Party. The American Vegetarian Party was formed in 1947. One of the party's mottos was "Be Kind to Animals By Not Eating Them."

Time to Vote!

On Election Day, people vote in their own states. Schools and government offices may be closed. Voters may be able to leave work to vote. States tell people where they can vote. These places are called **polling places**. A person's polling place is based on where they live.

Voters went to their polling place at a community center in 2018.

Each state picks where the polling places are located. In large cities, polling places are usually near busy neighborhoods or major subway or bus routes. Libraries, churches, and school gyms are also common voting spots.

STRANGE POLLING PLACES

Laundromats, lifeguard stations, appliance stores, and even a Chinese restaurant have been used as polling places. In 2018, people in California had to go to a funeral home to vote.

Now that you know where to go, it's time to vote. Not so fast. Voters have to be registered. Before or on Election Day, voters are asked to fill out a form. This form asks for the voter's name, address, age, and citizenship status. People can register in person. They can also register by mail or online before the election.

What happens if you can't make it to your polling place? Voters can vote early by using an absentee **ballot**. Absentee ballots are accepted by mail and in person. You can even have someone pick up your ballot and deliver it for you. People serving in the military often vote with absentee ballots.

FACT: Astronauts can vote online. David Wolf was the first astronaut to vote from space.

When You Can't Vote Yet

You may not be old enough to vote yet. But it is still important to know what's going on during elections. Follow TV reports, read candidate comments online, watch debates on TV, and talk with your family and friends. Develop your own opinions about the candidates and the issues.

Read online comments about your favorite candidate.

Talk to others about issues that are important to you during an election.

Issues like taxes and healthcare may not seem important to you now. But there are some topics you and other future voters should think about. You may be interested in a candidate's views on the environment, climate change, or college education. These things may affect you in the years ahead.

Talk to your teacher about using class time to talk about elections. See what other students in your class think about the issues. Some schools even hold mock elections, where students can vote for who they think should win. Compare your school's results to the votes on election night.

Do you want to help your candidate? Wear a T-shirt that supports him or her. Talk to your parents about raising money for your candidate. They can help you organize a car wash or bake sale. Give the money you raise to the candidate's campaign. Ask your parents to take you with them to a political rally. You could also write a letter or email to the candidate you support.

Students can attend rallies for a presidential candidate..

Helping with a campaign is one way for a student to get involved.

Talk to the voters you know, such as your family members, friends, and neighbors. Explain to them how important it is to vote. Ask them who they support and why. Get information from people with different political views. It's important to see all sides of an issue.

On Election Day, ask a parent to take you to the polling place when they vote. You can see what voting is like up close. Ask your parents questions afterward. Watch the election results on TV or online to see how your candidate did.

Voting is important. Voters can speak up and let their opinions be heard. It gives us the power to change what we don't like in our government and community. Voting matters!

Voters went to their polling place on Election Day in 2012.

A boy stood near a voting booth in California.

Glossary

amendment (uh-MEND-muhnt)—a change made to a law or legal document

ballot (BAH-let)—paper or card used to vote in an election

campaign (kam-PAYN)—organized actions and events with a specific goal, such as being elected

candidate (KAN-duh-dayt)—a person who runs for office

citizen (SI-tuh-zuhn)—a member of a country or state who has the right to live there

Congress (KAHN-gruhs)—the part of the United States government that makes laws; Congress is made up of the Senate and the House of Representatives

Constitution (kahn-stuh-TOO-shun)—the written system of laws in a country that state the rights of people

debate (di-BAYT)—discussion with sides with different views

democracy (di-MAH-kruh-see)—a form of government in which the people elect their leaders

fund-raiser (FUHND-ray-zehr)—an event to raise money for a cause or project

polling place (POHL-ing PLAYSS)—the place where people vote in an election

right (RITE)—something that the law says you can have or do

Read More

Mara, Wil. Voting: *A Citizen's Guide*. Ann Arbor, MI: Cherry Lake Publishing, 2017.

Shamir, Ruby. *What's the Big Deal About Elections?* New York, Philomel Books, 2018.

Small, Cathleen. *Elections and Voting.* New York: Lucent Press, 2019.

Internet Sites

How Voting Works
https://www.ducksters.com/history/us_government_voting.php

Kids Voting
https://kidsvotingusa.org/

Voting in the United States
https://www.scholastic.com/teachers/articles/teaching-content/voting-united-states/

Index

absentee ballots, 23

campaigns, 15, 26
candidates, 14, 15, 16, 17, 18, 24, 25, 26, 28
Congress, 13
    representatives, 8, 13
    senators, 8, 13

debates, 17, 24
democracy, 5

Election Day, 12, 20, 22, 28
elections, 4, 9, 12, 13, 14, 22, 24, 26, 28
    local elections, 10
    mock elections, 26
    national elections, 12
    state elections, 11

fund-raisers, 15

political parties, 18
polling places, 20, 21, 23, 28
presidents, 8, 12

rallies, 15, 26
registering, 22
rights, 5, 6

U.S. Constitution, 5, 6
    15th Amendment, 6
    19th Amendment, 6